L.W.

God Bless You!!!

Ray Hampton II

3-24-96

BUILDING LEADERS for EVANGELISM

RAY HAMPTON

WinePress Publishing Mukilteo, WA 98275

Building Leaders for Evangelism
Copyright © 1996 Ray Hampton
Published by WinePress Publishing
PO Box 1406, Mukilteo, WA 98275

All rights reserved. No part of this publication may be reproduced, stored in a retrieval system or transmitted in any way by any means, electronic, mechanical, photocopy, recording or otherwise, without the prior permission of the publisher, except as provided by USA copyright law.

All Scripture quotations are taken from the *New King James Version* of the Bible. Copyright © 1979, 1980, 1982, Thomas Nelson, Inc., Publishers.

Printed in Canada on recycled paper.

ISBN 1-883893-29-1

To order additional copies of
Building Leaders For Evangelism
please send $9.95* + $2.00 for shipping and handling to:

Pastor Ray Hampton
PO Box 1363
Lynnwood, WA 98046

Building Leaders For Evangelism
can also be purchased as a four cassette tape series for only $15.00* + $3.50 for shipping and handling.

*Washington Residents add 7.8% sales tax

In Memory of

Isaiah Cornelius Hampton

August 7, 1991 to January 19, 1992

Acknowledgements

To the Father, the Son and the Holy Spirit without whom this book would not have been possible.

I give acknowledgment and express my appreciation and love to my wife Julia who has labored continuously by my side for many years. You have been an inspiration to me and birthed five wonderful children. With you standing by my side, the struggles of life have seemed easier.

"He who finds a wife finds a good thing and obtains favor from the Lord." Proverbs 18:22

Foreword
by Tim Storey

I am truly excited about what God is doing throughout the earth in the area of soul winning. The Bible says He that winneth souls is wise (Proverbs 11:30). That is why I am thrilled about the wise book by Ray Hampton on the subject of soul winning! Ray Hampton gives us practical insights, plus exciting revelation on how to truly act our Christianity by becoming a force on the earth. Ray Hampton has a terrific testimony of what God has done for him. And because of God's delivering power in his own life, he has an incredible passion to see God deliver other people in need. This book will challenge and inspire you and send you forth into wise living.

About the Author

Pastor Ray Hampton III was born in Oahu, Hawaii, on October 8, 1964. He is the son of Pastor Raymond Hampton, Jr. and Mrs. Jacqueline Hampton. He accepted Christ on Friday, September 27, 1985. His first sermon was preached on September 15, 1989 and he received his license to preach in December 1990 from the Power House Church of God in Christ, Pastor Henry Jenkins, Sr. and District Missionary Rubie Jenkins. Pastor Ray Hampton was ordained on November 29, 1992 under the administration of Bishop T. L. Westbrook.

He is married to Julia Hampton and is the father of Trenecsia Nacole, Raymond IV, Michael James, Catrena Sharde and the late Isaiah Cornelius. Pastor Ray was senior pastor of Safe In His Arms Christian Center which he began with 14 members. God kept blessing him. He has also served as pastor of evangelism and church evangelist of Silver Lake Chapel in Everett, Washington, where Pastor Vince and Jodiann Schott are the senior pastors.

As the church evangelist of more than a 2,300 member congregation, Pastor Ray Hampton is excited about the number of people who have come off the streets to Silver Lake Chapel. Pastor Ray Hampton III is known across the United States for his powerful street ministry. He attended Edmonds Community College and Washington State University from 1984 to 1990 and is currently an instructor on staff at Silver Lake Bible College.

Pastor Ray Hampton has also made guest appearances on local Northwest TV and radio stations such as KCIS, KCMS and Trinity Broadcasting Network. He is very visible in the state of Washington speaking on panels concerning minorities, youth, Christian-related issues, evangelism and effective leadership. He also serves as chaplain for Snohomish County Corrections and professional athletic teams in the state.

Introduction

A disciple is a student of a teacher who adopts the teaching of his teacher. The Jews considered themselves to be ultimately disciples of Moses. "Then they hurled insults at him and said, You are this fellow's disciple! We are disciples of Moses." (John 9:28)

John the Baptist also had disciples. "The next day John was there again with two of his disciples." (John 1:35)

A good disciple will practice what he is taught after receiving what is caught. For you to be an effective disciple you need to pay close attention to what you are taught, so you can receive the full knowledge of the ministry, business or marriage that is waiting for you to step up and grab it.

You need to always ask questions. The most foolish questions are the ones never asked. "One day Jesus was praying in a certain place. When He finished, one of his disciples said to Him, 'Lord teach us to pray just as John taught his disciples.'" (Luke 11:1) If you do not ask how to do something you will not know how to do it. If you talk too much you will not grasp what is being taught.

Most people who are trying to learn from a teacher or a leader are open-minded. Most closed-minded people can be trained but are hard to train because of two main reasons: religion and tradition. These two words have kept most people from reaching their maximum potential of what God has for them. "See to it that no one takes you captive through hollow and deceptive philosophy, which depends on human tradition and the basic principles of this world rather than Christ." (Colossians 2:8)

Remember these steps! You should always be quick to listen, slow to speak, slow to anger; do not be religious and stay away from tradition. This book will also focus on what it takes to deliver your vision and how to build a successful leadership team. "There are many desires in one's heart but only the purpose of the Lord will be revealed." (Proverbs 19:21) There are a lot of people trying to do a lot of things. Most of those things are just desires or dreams. A desire without a purpose is just a desire and a dream without a vision is just a dream. The key to reaching the potential that God has for you is not to be the greatest leader but the greatest servant. Jesus is a good leader, but He is also a great servant. A good follower of a servant of the Gospel will always be a great leader of the Gospel.

CHAPTER ONE

Pregnant with a Vision

"There are many plans in a man's heart, nevertheless the Lord's council will stand."

(Proverbs 19:21)

A lot of people are disturbed in their minds about what their purpose or calling is in life. They make bad financial and timing decisions. If we would consult God through prayer and fasting, a lot of wasted time could be saved. People act on their desires because they are trying to find their purpose in life. Not knowing your purpose for life could cause you to go through a lot of desires. The best steps to find out your purpose and calling for life is to:

1. Pray
2. Fast
3. Let the Holy Spirit lead and guide you
4. Do not share your vision with everybody
5. Know when the opportunity comes.

Do you ever have any doubt about what is your purpose or calling for life? The idea that you doubt normally is your calling most of the time. Most people fail in life because of no vision. The Bible says, "Where there is no vision people perish."

I would like to tell you where there is a vision you will flourish. You have to know where you are headed in life so you can lead someone else to success and help pull them out of the pit of failure. This is called the "process to success."

"If a blind man leads a blind man, both will fall into a pit." (Matthew 15:14) I would like to challenge you right now to get ready, close your eyes and as you do ask God to show you what is stopping you from reaching your maximum potential in what God has called you to do. And He will do it.

You cannot be persuaded in another person's anointing or purpose in life, or take their anointing. You need to believe in yourself and work on your own anointing. A lot of other men can say nice things about my wife and treat her like a princess, but to me she is my queen. You see, other people will always admire things that God has blessed you with, such as: church, ministries, home, car, etc. If people say that they would like to have the things or wife that I have, my response to them is that they might be able to find something similar, but they cannot have mine, because God blessed me with it. Sometimes people get discouraged because their churches and ministries are not growing. The husband or the wife is losing interest in their spouse or they do not want to continue a business venture they started. Most of this is due to jealousy and not spending enough time in what God had originally told you to do. The grass may look greener on the other side, but that is only because you are not taking care of your own lawn.

You need to start fertilizing the church where you are the pastor, the ministry that you are over and the home that you live in before you can effectively tell someone else how God has blessed you. "But seek first the Kingdom of God and his righteousness, and all these things shall be added to you." (Matthew 6:33)

The key to a successful church, ministry or home is not to seek other people's programs because God does not bless programs, He only blesses people. How does He bless people? Through seeking Him. The more you pray and seek God for direction the more you will see things turn around. "When prayers go up, blessings come down." You should not worry about or listen to people who are always trying to put a negative spirit on you of "you will never do it, or it's not in you." God wants you to run and possess the land!

"Do you not know that those who run in a race all run, but one receives the prize? Run in such a way that you may obtain it. And everyone who competes for the prize is temperate in all things. Now they do it to obtain a perishable crown, but we for an imperishable crown. Therfore I run thus: not with uncertainty. Thus I fight: not as one who beats the air. But I discipline my body my body and bring it in to subjection, lest, when I have preached to others, I myself should become disqualified." (I Corinthians 9:24-27)

God has given everyone some type of dream. Some people's dream might be to start a restaurant or daycare. For others it might be to write your first book or produce a compact disc in the ministry of music. Whatever it is, I am absolutely positive that within you there is something just waiting to get out. But only God and you know what it is. The only way you are going to deliver the dream that is pregnant within you is to go into training.

The most frequently asked question is, "How do I go into training and prepare myself?" A football player cannot just sit around and eat ribs and fried chicken in the off season. He needs to start going to the gym to prepare himself for the next season by eating right, lifting weights and running so many miles every day. If your dream is to pastor a successful and growing church, you need to turn that dream into a vision and go into strict training to prepare yourself. You need to plant yourself around other successful pastors in the ministry, lead a successful godly home, have a daily prayer life, a fasting life, consistently study the Scriptures and, "Do not conform to this world, but be transformed by the renewing of your mind, that you may prove what is that good and acceptable and perfect will of God." (Romans 12:2)

Do not deliver your vision just so you can show everybody that you can grow the biggest church, make the most money through your business or produce a compact disc that is number one on the charts. If it is not for the glory of God to win souls for the kingdom, it is a crown of vanity. When you get out of the way and put God first and let Him build your church, business or ministry, you will automatically see supernatural blessings start to happen.

Keeping Your Dream Alive

"Now Joseph dreamed a dream, and he told it to his brothers; and they hated him even more." (Genesis 37:5)

Whenever you start dreaming about something that is going to better your future, be careful that you do not tell everyone your God-given dreams. Only tell your prayer partners, leadership team and spouse so you can stay tuned-in to what God is speaking to you.

So he said to them, "Please hear this dream which I have dreamed: And indeed your sheaves stood all around and bowed down to my sheaf." And his brothers said to him, "Shall you indeed reign over us? or shall you indeed have dominion over us? So they hated him even more for his dreams and for his words." (Genesis 37:6-8)

Be careful who you tell your dream to because they might think that you are trying to take their position. The only reason most people get upset anyway is because of their insecurity.

Everybody can have a dream but without a vision it is just a dream. The definition of a dream is "a series of thoughts, images or emotions occurring during sleep." A vision is "something that is seen in a dream or a supernatural appearance that brings about a revelation."

"Then they said to one another, look this dreamer is coming! Come therefore, let us now kill him and cast him into some pit; and we shall say, some wild beast has devoured him. We shall see what will become of his dreams!" (Genesis 37:19-20)

Keep your dreams and visions to yourself because until it comes to pass most people will try to sow a seed of doubt in your path. When the vision that God gave you finally comes to pass, you do not have to say a word such as, "I told you so," to the people who tried to sow a seed of doubt. The manifestation and fruit of your vision will speak for itself.

There are three major problems people have with their vision:

1. Some people will start the vision that God has given them and somewhere along the road to success their money starts to run out or that seed of doubt that someone planted at the conception of the vision starts to rise in their spirit. They may decide to **abort the vision**. They just drop it.

2. Some people will carry the vision that God has given them and somewhere along the road to success they just run around doing a bunch of godly things for the vision. But, they

are not sitting, lying or kneeling down in prayer so God can spiritually bring it together. They end up **miscarrying the vision**.

3. Some people will take care of the vision that God has given them for months, even years, and through frustration and loneliness they decide to **adopt the vision out**, wanting it back later in life.

The best way to deliver your vision is to get some help. Many people have the tools to pastor their church or direct their business, but they still lack consistency. To be able to reach your maximum potential, you need to fill the area where you are lacking. The majority of pastors who start churches start with only a handful of people. They move from building to building, never staying long enough in one place to build real relationships in the community. Why does this happen? The are unstable, have a lack of focus or they have too much zeal. "Zeal without knowledge is not good."

One of the hardest things for pastors who pioneer churches to do is to get their congregation count up to 100. Some pastors have been pastoring for five, ten or 15 years and still have not tapped into the harvest. I believe this is not because they are bad people, but because they need to reach out and get some help.

Here are a few simple ideas I have given to pastors which have caused their churches to increase in size:

Majority, not minority.

Do not have a bunch of empty folding chairs out while the service is going on because people like to feel like the majority, not the minority. That's why churches that are 100, 200 and 300 or more can take off in growth spurts. People bring people. Where people are blessed you will always see lots of activities and programs for the whole family. If you only have 50 people in your church, make them feel like they are the majority on Sundays, not the minority.

Do not be late.

The second problem that will keep people from coming to a church is that most new churches don't have a starting time. They are always waiting for more people to come and their musicians to get ready. I do not care who is there, if 11 a.m. is the starting time and as long as you are there, you need to start! "Faith is the substance of things hoped for, the evidence of things not seen." (Hebrews 11:1)

If you believe and see the multitudes coming to your church it will happen. But you have to start on time. I do not care who is there. Jesus said, "For where two or three are gathered together in My Name, I am there in the midst of them." (Matthew18:20)

If you stop worrying about who is not there and worry about who is there, God will bless you. "You were faithful over a few things, I will make you ruler over many things." (Matthew 25:21)

If you are lacking in these areas, stop refusing to push out your vision. Most ministries and churches have dilated to 10 centimeters, but refuse to push to the next level. No where in history will you find a woman who has been pregnant forever, so why do most churches "stay pregnant?" I believe it is because they are having a hard time pushing out to the next level. I believe that this can be done with a human forceps delivery. This can be accomplished by praying and fasting for God to send someone into your life to mentor you so you can tap into your destiny.

CHAPTER TWO

Building a Leadership Team

The following are nine qualities of leadership:

1. You have to be a fighter.

"Fight the good fight of faith, lay hold on eternal life to which you were also called and have confessed the good confession in the presence of many witnesses." (I Timothy 6:12)

2. Have a servant's heart.

"His Lord said to him, 'Well done good and faithful servant; you were faithful over a few things, I will make you ruler over many things. Enter into the joy of your Lord.'" (Matthew 25:21)

3. Have a spiritual hunger.

"Blessed are those who hunger and thirst for righteousness, for they shall be filled." (Matthew 5:6)

4. Stop spending time with books about the Bible and spend more time with the Bible.

"Be diligent to present yourself approved to God, a worker who does not need to be ashamed, rightly dividing the Word of truth." (II Timothy 2:15)

5. Accept correction.

"My son, do not despise the chastening of the Lord, nor detest his correction; for whom the Lord loves He corrects." (Proverbs 3:11-12a)

6. Put your faith in God.

"Now faith is the substance of things hoped for, the evidence (realization and confidence) of things not seen." (Hewbrews 11:1)

"For we walk by faith, not by sight." (II Corinthians 5:7)

7. Study Biblical doctrine.

"All Scripture is given by inspiration of God, and is profitable for doctrine, for reproof, for correction, for instruction (training or discipline) in righteousness, that the man of God may be complete, thoroughly equipped for every good work." (II Timothy 3:16-17)

8. Have your family in order.

"...but as for me and my house, we will serve the Lord." (Joshua 24:15b)

9. You cannot quit.

"Being confident of this very thing, that He who has begun a good work in you will complete it until the day of Jesus Christ." (Philippians 1:6)

Stop Complaining

The reason most pastor's churches or ministries are not growing could be because they complain. They complain, complain and complain about why people keep leaving their church or why people want them to do so much for them because it is wearing them out. I believe that the reason why some churches or ministries continue to grow and others don't is not because they do not fast or pray, but simply because one man cannot pastor a multitude of people by himself. Perhaps a maximum (small or none) but never a multitude (a lot or larger). That is why it is important to build a leadership team. In order for your church or ministry to have successful growth, you have to stop complaining.

"Now Moses heard the people weeping throughout their families, everyone at the door of his tent; and the anger of the Lord was greatly aroused; Moses also was displeased. So Moses said to the Lord, 'Why have you afflicted your servant? And why have I not found favor in your sight, that you have laid the burden of all these people on me?'" (Numbers 11:10-11)

Most pastors are going through the same thing that Moses was going through, hearing the problems and frustration of the people in their churches. Some people in the congregation are saying that there is not enough worship music and others are saying there is too much. As a pastor who oversees a tremendous amount of food and a large staff for the church food bank, I can clearly understand how Moses felt. There have been a lot of times the food bank was low on food, but that did not change the demand by people for food. I have been so angry at times because there have been hundreds of people in line waiting for food, complaining about their circumstances, some even weeping.Sometimes I have felt like crying out to the Lord like Moses did,"Why have you afflicted your servant and why have you laid the burden of all these people on me?"

As much as I think that I will not be able to meet the needs of the people, God always supplies the need in time. In Numbers 11:13, Moses asks a question, "Where am I to get meat to give to all these people?"

Most pastors are asking God similar questions today. "How do I start a children's church for all the children? Home groups for all the people? Food bank to serve? Street ministry to minister?" The answer is very simple. **Get some help**! "And so it was, on the next day, that Moses sat down to judge the people; and the people stood before Moses from morning until evening." (Exodus 18:13)

This is still happening today. Pastors and leadership are still trying to answer all the questions of the congregation, meeting with everybody all day long and trying to solve everyone's problems. It is true that as a pastor or leader you are called to serve the people. But if you cannot pastor, lead and serve your family first, you will have problems. "For what is a man profited if he gains the whole world, and loses his own soul?" (Matthew 16:26)

"For if a man does not know how to rule his own house, how will he take care of the church of God?" (I Timothy 3:5) You have to have a balance in ministry. Too much ministry outside the home can even make your spouse jealous of your second girlfriend or boyfriend, which is the ministry. This is why you need to build a team.

"So when Moses' father-in-law saw all that he did for the people, he said, 'What is this thing that you are doing for the people? Why do you alone sit (as judge), and all the people stand before you from morning until evening.' And Moses said to his father-in-law, 'Because the people come to me to inquire of God. When they have a difficulty (dispute) they come to me, and I judge between one and another; and I make known the statues of God and His laws.'" (Exodus 18:14-16)

Many pastors are doing this very same thing. They are trying to answer the difficult questions of the people and are getting involved in every dispute between people and their church. As a pastor, I have come to the conclusion that if people want to be helped, they first have to be willing to confess their faults in the problem. If they cannot, then our meeting is over. It is very important to realize that as pastors and leaders, you only have so much good fuel to lead your church or ministries. If you let everyone drain you of your fuel too soon, you will never have enough for the long trip of ministry. You will constantly be getting off on every exit of counseling, out of fuel. The best way to reserve your fuel for longevity in ministry is to have multiple fuel tanks on your team. Then they can take some of the load off you as leader to counsel more people and cover more areas of ministry in your church or business. "So Moses' father-in-law said to him, 'The thing that you do is not good. Both you and these people who are with you will surely wear yourselves out. For this thing is too much for you, you are not able to perform it by yourself.'" (Exodus 18:17-18)

You can clearly see from Scripture that trying to be the main captain of the boat will wear you out. Exodus 18:18 shows why new or pioneer churches go through so much confusion, always changing locations, behind in their bills and mad because nobody will come to their church. It's because leaders do not build their teams as they grow. That's why the Scripture says, "Both you and these people (the congregation) who are with you will surely wear yourselves out." This doesn't refer to multiple staff, but only talks about the one person trying to do and have the congregation do everything. The

Scripture confirms this at the end saying, "For this thing is too much for you; you are not able to perform it by yourself."

Building Your Staff

"Listen now to My voice; I will give you counsel, and God be with you: stand before God for the people, so that you may bring the difficulties to God." (Exodus 18:19)

1. If you are the leader of your church or ministry, don't complain about everyone's problems before you even counsel them; if you absolutely have to counsel them, take it to God in prayer.

"And you shall teach them the statues and the laws, and show them the way in which they must walk and the work they must do." (Exodus 18:20)

2. Every leader needs to teach and show their congregation or team the way to be a Christian (Christ-like), according to sound biblical doctrine.

"Moreover you shall select from all the people able men, such as fear God, men of truth, hating covetousness; and place such over them to be rulers to thousands, rulers of hundreds, rulers of fifties and rulers of ten." (Exodus 18:21)

3.   Every leader needs to be able to select people who have a heart for the ministry area you are asking them to do, so they will be able to raise up leaders with the same heart.

"And let them judge the people at all times. Then it will be that every great matter they shall bring to you, but every small matter they themselves shall judge. So it will be easier for you, for they will bear the burden with you." (Exodus 18:22)

4.   There are two ways to look at a leader. Some people are leaders over leaders and some are leaders over workers. This portion of Scripture is saying let your leaders over their workers take care of all the problems in their ministry areas and church. If the problem is too great, they need to come to the senior leader for help. Then it is the senior leader's responsibility to take it to God in prayer since it is a difficult problem (Exodus 18:19). No senior leader should have to carry the load of their church, ministry or business by themselves. All the leaders should bear it together until God gives the senior leader the solution to the problem. "If you do this thing and God so commands you, then you will be able to endure, and all this people will also go their place in peace."(Exodus 18:23)

5. If you build your ministry team God's way and not your way, you will have longevity in ministry. If you choose not to, you will be just another ministry—"just hanging on 'til Jesus comes." You need to do more than hang on. You need to "stay on 'til Jesus comes." Anything that hangs you will kill you. But if you're staying on something it will bring you success because you have control of it. Do you want to just hang on so the devil can tighten the rope and choke you? Why not stay somewhere and have longevity and success and tighten up your rope and choke all the hell out of the devil?

Choosing Your Volunteers

As you build your team of volunteers, it is very important that you take care of them. Most churches or ministries build great teams, but they do not take care of them. Building a successful team that lasts is the same way you build a successful marriage that lasts.

Before you start to build your ministry team, you first have to see the type of quality within that person which you are looking for. You do not have to see the whole picture at first, but if you can see a preview of the seed that is planted in that person, that is all you need. After finding a team member you need to do the same thing as you did when finding a spouse. Go on "multiple dates" to learn more about their character. As you learn about their character you will soon know their actions which will show you their personality.

These three things are very important in a marriage because the character of the person will show you how they carry themselves. Their actions will tell you how they solve problems. Their personality will tell you ultimately what kind of team person they will be.

After dating for a season, then it is time to ask them to join your team. This is what you call a proposal. Most people will tell you "let me pray about it and I'll get back to you this week." Most volunteers who don't want to work in the particular ministry area will not spend time with you talking about it (dating). They will normally make excuses why they cannot meet with you. But if they have spent time with you, then they are interested. So normally when they tell you they are going to get back to you, the answer is yes! In marriage this is called engagement. When getting engaged to a future team member it is very important to set a date when the person will start their first ministry work date, in other words this is when you will get "married." It is so important to pick your team like you would a marriage partner because these will be the people who will help you succeed. I would not be the leader, husband or father that I am today if I did not have a wonderful wife named Julia to compliment me. Remember before you can have a proposal, engagement and marriage make sure you have the love and trust of your future team members because you will be together for a long time. Do not set yourself up for a divorce.

Taking Care of Your Volunteers

There are a lot of ways to take care of your volunteers for their service of work. Most volunteers on your team are mothers with children who also work full-time jobs or fathers who have a lot of responsibility on their secular jobs which cause them to work overtime. Some are single adults who are working and going to college to receive a higher education. You have to understand that all of your volunteers have other things to do besides work with you. If you take care of your volunteers they will take care of you. The problem is that most leaders don't know how to take care of their volunteers. I would like to show you some tools that I use to "pay" my volunteers.

1. A monthly thank-you letter
2. A quarterly lunch or dinner
3. Time spent with ministry leaders

4. Remembering their birthday and anniver-
    sary with a card
5. Certificates of appreciation
6. Time off given so they won't burn out

These are just a few ways you can say thank-you to your volunteers. If you have other ideas put those into your ministry because, remember, if you do not take care of them, they will not take care of you.

CHAPTER THREE

Basic Forerunner Evangelism

There are a lot of people sitting in congregations or pacing the floor and thinking about what kind of program they can start in their church that will bring multitudes of people in from their community or city. I have come to realize that this concept of starting program after program will not bring people into your church. Most churches are starting children's programs but have no children's workers. Others are starting youth programs but have no youth workers. Some are even trying to lead programs who don't have leadership qualities or capabilities. In other words, they are ignorant leaders—which means they have a lack of knowledge in leading people. This brings me to a very important conclusion. If you cannot lead people, how can you start a program to get people to come to your church? The reason why people are not coming to your church is not because you did not have a program but because God does not bless programs alone, He blesses people. If the people, workers and leaders are blessed the programs will always be blessed. When the workers and the leaders have started to follow the doctrines of the Bible and not the doctrines of man, evangelism can be "basic, not hard." There are at least four basic principles you should have before going out into the community or city to evangelize.

1. You have to be saved.

"That if you confess with your mouth the Lord Jesus and believe in your heart that God has raised Him from the dead, you will be saved." Romans 10:9

2. You have to believe in Jesus.

"For God so loved the world that He gave His only begotten Son, that whoever believes in Him should not perish but have everlasting life." (John 3:16)

3. Be redeemed by His blood.

"Knowing that you were not redeemed with corruptible things, like silver or gold, from your aimless conduct received by tradition from your fathers. But with the precious blood of Christ, as of a lamb without blemish and without spot." (I Peter1:18-19)

4. Believe that Jesus died on the cross.

"If you are the son of God come down from the cross."(Matthew 27:40)

One of the greatest similarities within each of these four principles is that in each one the main word has five letters.The following words **saved, Jesus, blood and cross** are key words that represent grace in our lives. Or five can mean incompletion,which is the other significance of the number five. In Ephesians 4:11-12 it says, "And He Himself gave some to be apostles, some prophets, some evangelists, and some pastors and teachers."

The reason why these gifts of offices were given to the church was not so everyone can be ineffective or broken down, but so Christians can be effective and built up. Verse 12 in this chapter proves this by saying, "For the equipping of the saints for the work of ministry, for the edifying (building up) of the body of Christ." Out of these five-fold ministries to the church, I would like to focus on the office of the evangelist.

Welcome to the Mission Field

As I travel around the United States to speak at churches on evangelism, I have noticed one thing most of the churches (not all, but most) have in common. They do not have an evangelism department, which means no pastor of evangelism in the church. The reason why most churches are not growing is not because the people don't love God or they are disobedient. Most senior pastors do want their church to grow, but all they ever tell the congregation every Sunday is, "Bring someone to church next Sunday."

The problem with this statement is that the majority of the congregation would love to bring someone to church but they don't know how to approach the person to invite them. So only a minority of the congregation end up bringing someone to the church. The majority does nothing. So the new person comes through the front door only to go out the back door. When the minority of the congregation invites people to church you will have growth spurts. But when the majority of the congregation invites people you will have growth pains. I do believe that most churches need to go back to B.A.S.I.C. evangelism. This means **Brother And Sister In Christ** evangelism.

As I have stated, most churches do not have an evangelism department. They only have missions departments supporting missionaries that they have sent out from the local church. I do believe that missions is important; however, I believe that most churches are **overseeing** the local community while they are flying **overseas**. It has always bothered me that we can go to Russia, Africa, Japan, Mexico, China, India, etc. and take lots of needed merchandise but cannot let our neighbor borrow the vacuum cleaner. How can we smuggle Bibles into China and not smuggle Bibles among our own families. It is very important on your air flight to the mission field that when you look out of the window of the plane that you make sure you are not "flying over" the mission field trying to get to the mission field.

Basic Instructions

There are at least three basic instructions to remember when you are evangelizing on the streets.

1. Preach biblically sound doctrine.

"Remain in Ephesus that you may charge some that they teach no other doctrine." (I Timothy 1:3)

When you are witnessing to someone or a crowd of people never speak above your own experience. Just keep your conversation simple. Most Christians are ineffective in their witnessing because they are only talking about the doctrine of their church or denomination instead of talking about biblically sound doctrine. The easiest way to remember what to do when you are witnessing is to remember the word **preach**.

*   First you have to PREACH to the person.
*   Second you need to REACH for the person.
*   You can only witness to EACH person at a time.
*   If you follow these steps you will have good P.R. (public relations) in your community, city, state and world.

PREACH

REACH

EACH

2. You should also avoid false teaching.

"O Timothy! Guard what was committed to your trust, avoiding the profane and vain babblings and contradictions of what is falsely called knowledge, by professing it some have strayed concerning the faith. Grace be with you. Amen." (I Timothy 6:20-21)

Paul told Timothy to avoid false teaching. Praise the Lord! If more Christians would study their own Bible instead of someone else's Bible I believe that we would see more people on track instead of off the track. The average Christian who goes witnessing on the job in the mall or on the streets always starts out like a train taking off from the railroad station. They go from city to city dropping off people. But sometimes they derail. Now, as you know, a Christian is not a train. But a lot of energetic, ignorant (lack of knowledge) Christians think they have the same power two weeks after they get saved to take off and go city to city. I believe the most important thing a young, or ignorant Christian can do is to be a learner or a disciple of a leader so they do not derail off the track to religious teachings, but stay on the course and have a relationship with Jesus.

3. You need to be diligent and faithful.

"Preach the word! Be ready in season and out of season.Convince, rebuke, exhort with longsuffering and teaching. For the time will come when they will not endure sound doctrine, but according to their own desires, because they have itching ears,they will heap up for themselves teachers. And they will turn their ears away from the truth, and be turned aside to fables.But you be watchful in all things, endure afflictions, do the work of an evangelist, fulfill your ministry." (II Timothy 4:2-5)

If you are absolutely positive that you have accepted Christ in your life and you are a Christian, why are you just going to church without bringing someone or witnessing to someone before you go? The beginning of verse two says "Preach the word." The first thing you should do when you become a Christian is "preach the word." Now I know most Christians would probably say, "How can I preach the word when I am not a pastor or evangelist?" You might not have a calling on your life of the office of pastor or evangelist, but you do have a calling on your life to be a witness or a minister of the gospel, that is tell about the good news. Here are just a few Scriptures to remind you that you need to get up and "go preach the word."

"But you shall receive power when the Holy Spirit has come upon you: and you shall be witnesses to me in Jerusalem, and in all Judea and Samaria, and to the end of the earth." (Acts 1:8)

Do you have the Holy Spirit on you? Many Christians say they are filled with the Spirit of Christ but nothing effective ever comes out of their mouths to let you know. In the book of Acts you knew when people were filled with the Spirit. They spoke in tongues, prophesied and spoke with boldness. The problem with most Christians is that they might have the Spirit of Christ in them, but they need to be filled with the Spirit so it can be on them, flowing out of their mouths and lives. A good example of this is a glass of water. You can have water in the glass (the Spirit in you) but when you consistently fill the water glass it will flow on and out of it (the Spirit on you and out of you).

Acts 1:8 sums all of this up by saying that if you have the Spirit of Christ upon you (up on you) you will not be powerless but have power, not sit on a church pew or at home all day but you will be an effective witness for Jesus.

"And we know that all things work together for good to those who love God, to those who are the called according to His purpose." (Romans 8:28)

The reason you have a good job is not only for your purpose.

The reason you have a good marriage is not only for your purpose. The reason why your bank account has money is not only for your purpose. The reason why none of your children are in jail is not for your purpose. The reason why you are not on welfare is not only for your purpose. The reason why your church is growing is not only for your purpose. The reason why your ministry is growing is not only for your purpose.

I could keep on going all day long, but the main reason why these blessings are happening in your life is not for you to get the glory and say "Look what I have done," but to give all the glory and thanks to God. Every blessing that happens in your life will always be a witness to someone else. There is an old saying that is still very effective today: "you might be the only Bible somebody reads." In other words, you are a witness to someone in everything you do. You need to make sure it is an effective witness for Jesus and not an uneffective witness for Him.

Basic International Tools

There are a lot of churches and ministries trying to use every tool possible to effectively reach people in their community and city, but I feel the most effective tool to use is one that is non-religious and simple. Before I go on the streets to witness, I always pray for divine appointments. "Lord where do you want me to go and what approach do you want me to take?" Even though the Holy Spirit sometimes has me go to different areas in the city, He always has me use two of the same tools. I personally have not had to put happy wigs on people to make them happy or dancing shoes to make them dance. What the Holy Spirit has led to do is two things: serve good food and have good music.

Food

It does not matter what country a person is from. One thing we all have in common is that everyone is capable of eating. I have taken a variety of food which is quick and handy to serve out on the streets, such as peanut butter and jelly sandwiches, hot dogs, potato chips, cookies, cocoa and juice. It is always a great idea to prepare sandwiches before you even go out to the streets.

I have found that the fastest way to pass out food on the streets is to put it in lunch sacks and hand them out one by one. There have been thousands of people fed on the streets in nightly street crusades with preaching going on and Bibles being handed out. I have personally been criticized for the way I have been handing out food on the streets. It has been said that I am tricking people into getting saved or I am putting out false advertisement. I first want to say that passing out food is not a trick, it is real. I know this because I see it, smell it and eat it. I know it is not false advertisement because I always bring it. So what is the problem?

I am so glad that Jesus did not tell Christians to go out and be religious but to go build relationships. To the people who tell me to not take food on the streets, I say don't take your fishing pole or bait when you go fishing. Just sit there and wait for the fish to jump in your lap. I am so glad that Jesus said, "Follow me, and I will make you fishers of men." (Matthew 4:19) Not fishers of complainers.

Music

Music is probably the second most international tool that can be used in every language because music is known as the universal language. You can have an English-speaking song playing on the streets with a non-English speaking Russian listening to it and feeling good. How can this happen? They might not understand the words but they definitely feel the beat. This brings me to a very important point I want to get in your spirit. There is nothing wrong with playing your 12-string guitar on the street corner singing, "I've got a river of life flowing out of me." But there is something wrong when nobody's listening to you. I do know that the word of the Lord does not return void, but I also know that the word of the Lord does not go out so people will **avoid** you.

"Then Peter said to them, 'Repent, and let everyone of you be baptized in the name of Jesus Christ for the remission of sins; and you shall receive the gift of the Holy Spirit. For the promise is to you and to your children, and to all who are afar off, as many as the Lord our God will call.' And with many other words he testified and exhorted them saying, 'Be saved from this perverse (crooked) generation.' Then those who gladly received his word were baptized; and that day about three thousand souls were added to them, praising God and having favor with all the people. And the Lord added to the church daily those who were being saved." (Acts 2:38-41,47)

From the look of this portion of Scripture, it sure does not sound or look to me that people were avoiding Peter but what they were doing was:

repenting of their sins,
receiving God's word,
rejoicing for their new transformation.

This is what needs to happen when you are playing music as a tool for witnessing on the streets. I have found out that it is the best to adjust your music to the crowd you are led to witness to.

Here are just a few examples of how I use music as a tool.

1. When witnessing to youth any rap, hip hop or rhythm and blues is always a plus. Just go to your local Bible book and music store and you will find it with gospel lyrics.

2. When witnessing to senior citizens any old hymn or spiritual will be fine. Don't push the issue of new sounds with a lot of fancy music. You will normally find this type of music on sale in your local Bible book and music store.

3. When you're witnessing to a general crowd, a mix of contemporary and good gospel choirs will always work for all types of people. You can also get this at your local Bible book and music store. It is waiting for you.

Remember that if you are going to play music that attracts people and guides them to the cross, play it but don't "foreplay with people if you are not going all the way!" If you never know what to say to attract other nationalities who don't speak English, remember that the word "hallelujah" is the same all over the world.

Forerunner Evangelism

A forerunner is one who prepares the way for something to happen or for something to come. Everyone has a forerunner. For instance, the denomination the Church of God in Christ was started by Bishop Charles Mason who was also the forerunner for the Assembly of God. Parents are forerunners for their children, preparing and teaching way for their children to have successful lives. As a forerunner you will not see instant salvations or miracles all the time when you are witnessing to people. It is very important that you remember that the word of God says, that "one plants, another person waters the plant, but God ultimately gives the increase." (I Corinthians 3:6)

So stop working. When you do your best, God will do the rest.

Whenever I go to the streets to witness, I always try to take someone with me. There have been times when I have gone out to the streets to witness alone, but it has always been better with another person.

"Two are better than one."(Ecclesiastes 4:9)

"But if he will not hear you, take with one one or two more that by the mouth of two or

three witnesses every word may be established."
(Matthew 18:16)

Even though the above and following portions of Scripture do not directly refer to evangelism, it does make one thing clear. Sometimes people will not listen to you when you are alone, but if you take someone else with you the chances of winning a sinner to Christ is excellent. **Do not go witnessing alone**.

"Again I say to you that if two of you agree on earth concerning anything that you ask, it will be done for you by my father in heaven. For where two or three are gathered together in my name, I am there in the midst of them." (Matthew 18:19-20)

There was a cartoon years ago called "Wonder Twins" and the greatest thing about this cartoon was that every time a job needed to be done there was togetherness between this brother and sister team. I remember one time as a child I was watching the Wonder Twins on a Saturday morning and their job was to put out a gigantic fire that was consuming a building. The way they accomplished this was by joining hands and shouting "Wonder Twins activate." The girl said, "Form of a bucket of water." The boy said, "Form of a ladder." And the bucket of water went hopping up the ladder to put out the fire. This is what you need to do when you are with someone out witnessing. Have togetherness.

"For this reason a man shall leave his father and mother and be joined to his wife, and the two shall become one flesh (an effective team)." (Ephesians 5:31)

Now we all know that this Scripture is talking about marriage and not evangelism, or at least I hope you know that. The reason why I have picked this Scripture is because it shows two people can be successful and have great miracles in their lives if they become one. From the passage we can see that having an effective team when witnessing is important.

When I think about what a forerunner is, the first example that comes to mind is the T.V. show "The Lone Ranger and Tonto." I remember how Tonto used to sit in the bar drinking and before he could even get one drink down someone was trying to pick a fight with him. But the odd thing about this fighting was that at the beginning of all the fights Tonto was always alone. Half-way through the fight, guess who shows up! Hioooo-Silver! You're right, the Lone Ranger shows up to help finish the fight and was gone before the fight was over.

This is an example of a forerunner who works in a team effort. In today's church world the associate pastors and support staff are the forerunners for the senior pastor. Most associate pastors always handle the majority of the church's problems before taking it to the senior pastors.

"Moreover you shall select from all the people able men, such as fear God, men of the truth...and let them judge the people at all times. Then it will be that every great matter they shall bring to you, but every small matter they themselves shall judge. So it will be easier for you, for they will bear the burden with you." (Exodus 18:21-22)

We can clearly see from this portion of Scripture how even associate pastors are forerunners. In Ecclesiastes 4:9-10 it says, "Two are better than one, because they have a good reward for their labor. For if they fall, one will lift up his companion. But woe to him who is alone when he falls, for he has no one to help him up." Two people can get better results than one when they are effectively working together.

John the Baptist was also a forerunner. In Matthew 3:11 he said, "I indeed baptize you with water unto repentance, but he who is coming after me is mightier than I, whose sandals I am not worthy to carry, he will baptize you with the Holy Spirit and fire." This means that John the Baptist was a forerunner for Jesus. As Tonto was to Lone Ranger and John the Baptist was to Jesus, the Christians (you) are the forerunners for the harvest.

"And Jesus went about all the cities and villages, teaching in their synagogues, preaching the gospel of the kingdom, and healing every sickness and every disease among the people. But when he saw the multitudes (harvest) he was moved with compassion for them becasue they were weary and scattered, like sheep having no shepherd. Then he (Jesus) said to his disciples (Christians) 'The harvest truly is plentiful but the laborers (Christians) are few. Therefore pray the Lord of the harvest to send out laborers (Christians) into his harvest.'"

The word Christian means to be Christ-like or like Christ and if we are going to follow in his footsteps we need to do the things that he did when reaching people. We need to be able and willing to:

teach anywhere,
preach the gospel of the kingdom,
heal every sickness and disease,
and be moved with compassion.

Jesus said there are a lot of people in the world who need to be reached. Guess who he wants to go out and get them? You! This means that Christians are forerunners for the harvest. So why don't more Christians get out of their seats and go to the streets and bring in the harvest?

CHAPTER FOUR

Street Gangs

Let's take a brief look at street gangs, since that is what you'll find when you start taking the Gospel to the streets.

GANG

Definition: A group of individuals who associate together for a common purpose, usually to the exclusion of others and participate in criminal and anti-social activity.

Street gangs may:
- claim turf
- have gang names (also called "sets")
- name their gangsters, called "monikers"
- have gang colors
- do graffiti
- use hand signs
- dress in a particular manner
- use tattoos.

Street gangs will participate in:

- criminal activity
- murder
- assault
- extortion
- robbery
- narcotics
- vehicle crimes
- intimidation

Gang related crime is a great threat to the community partly because of the gangster attitude. Assaults occur over turf, colors, hand signs, or as retaliation against another gang. There is an attitude of unity and "you can't stop us" combined with the desire to back up a fellow "homeboy." This leads to a continued retaliation and intimidation of victims and witnesses who may or may not be gang involved.

Gangster Characteristics

Monikers: T-Bone, B-Dog, T-Loco, Acc-Loc, 2-Smooth

Monikers are nicknames given to gang members by the gang set. These will often include the "loco" or "loc" which indicates how crazy the gangster is. The moniker may be some descriptive trait of the person. Monikers will often be found written in graffiti or on clothing such as ball caps or shirts. It might even be tattooed on the person's hand, arm, back or chest.

Initiation: "jumping in" or "jumping out," also known as "courting"

Gang member will refer to their fellow members as "homeboy" or "homey." They are "jumped in" to the gang usually by being beaten by several other members of the set. If a prospective member is beaten but not allowed in the gang following the beating, it is referred to as being "clowned." Getting out of the gang after being "jumped in" is very difficult or impossible, depending upon the gang.

The initiation process will often include the requirement for the prospective members to commit a certain crime such as an assault, theft or drive-by shooting. Female members are not immune from this process. They could be beaten or be required to have sex with several male members, or even be subject to a "gang rape."

Gang Structure

Original Gangster or "O.G."
These are the gangsters who start or are the founding members of a particular set. They are often viewed by the other members as having more authority in the set.

Hard-core members
These are deeply entrenched, 24-hour a day, 100% gangsters. They are in the gang for life, making it very difficult to work with these members. Success rate for permanently removing them from the gang is very low.

Members
They have been jumped into the gang but may not yet be as deeply committed. Chance for getting them out of the gang is slightly better than for the hard-core member.

Associates
They may hang out with, or associate with the gang members without actually having been jumped in. This stage has in the past has also been referred to as a "wanna-be" gangster. However, this term is no longer used since it is often not taken seriously. In reality, it is at this stage of involvement that a person can often be more dan-

gerous than a hard-core member since they are often more desperate to prove their worthiness of being in a gang.

Note: Crips and Bloods are not two gangs, they are like "nations" under which there are a number of "sets" or "hoods" which are the actual gangs. Crips outnumber Bloods approximately six to one.

Bloods/Piru

- Associate with the color red
- Hats: Phillies with "P" for Piru, Cardinals, UNLV, Chicago Bulls
- "C" is usually crossed out or the addition of "CK" for Crip killer
- Clothing: clothes are predominately red in color—scarves, rags (bandannas) shoe laces, national league attire, football, baseball, basketball.

Clothing worn by gangsters will be worn almost like a uniform. It may be clothing also popular with non-gang members. Alterations on this clothing should be noted for this may indicate gang affiliation.

- They will refer to fellow gang members as "blood."

- Will not use the letter "C" or will "X" it out. "CK" stands for Crip killer, "FK" stand for Folk (BGD) killer.

- Referred to as "slobs" by Crips

- Will align with other Blood sets and will not usually fight among themselves as do the Crips.

Crips

- Associate with the color blue (sometimes the color dark forest green in addition to blue).

- Clothing similar to that worn by the Bloods except in blue (i.e. Adidas, Nike, Georgetown).

- Refer to fellow gang members as "Cuz" or "Cousin."

- Will not use the letter "B" or will "X" it out. Will use a small "x" in place of dotting an i or a period.

- "BK" stands for "Blood killer" and "FK" stands for "Folk killer."

- Referred to as "Crabs", "E-Ricketts" or "C-Monster" by Bloods."

- Refer to gangs as "sets."

BGD/Folks — Black Gangster Disciples

- Associate with the color black, gray, or black and white.

- Clothing is similar to that worn by Crips and Bloods, predominantly black, gray and white (i.e. L.A. Raiders, and L.A. Kings) clothing, usually with gang logos on it.

Note: This clothing is also popular with Raiders and Kings' fans who are not necessarily gang involved.

- They consider themselves a local Seattle gang

- BGD's may be the fastest growing gang around. They differ from other gangs in that they consider themselves an organi zation and not a gang and have almost by-law type rules and a religious style of belief they follow.

- Membership is growing extremely fast

- Began in Chicago, where "Vice Lords" were their main rival gang

- Graffiti contains crowns, Stars of David, and pitchforks

- Referred to as "Bubble Gum Dummies" or "Folks" by rival gangs

Asian Gangs

Include Vietnamese, Cambodian, Laotian, Filipino and Chinese.

Crimes are: robberies—residential, business, vehicle thefts/prowls, intimidation, and extortion.

These gangs do not share many of the same characteristics as do the Crips and the Bloods, but their criminal activity clearly warrants the title of gang. However, many of the Asian gang sets are affiliating more often with the Blood gang sets.

O.L.B. — Oriental Local Blood

Characteristics:
- Often do not have colors
- Do not always have a gang name or "set"
- May have a gang leader
- Are generally very sophisticated
- Refer to other gang members as "friends"
- Tattoos may be the only identifier

These gangs are very mobile and commonly conduct crime sprees up and down the I-5 corridor.

Will commonly meet at billiard halls and will sometimes form a gang only for a particular crime and then disband. This is referred to as a "Hasty Gang."

Representation of current gang terminology and slang phrases:

Six-point star	BGD/Folk symbol
Five-point start	Vice Lord symbol
187	Code for murder
20 cents	$20 worth of cocaine (or other drugs)

Base head	Person hooked on cocaine
Beemer	BMW vehicle
Benzo	Mercedes Benz
BGD	Black Gangster Disciples
BK	Blood Killer
Blob	Crip nickname for Blood gang members
Blood	Piru/Non-Crip
Bo	Marijuana
Boned out	Quit, chicken out, left, leave
Book	Run, get away, leave
Break	Run, get away
Breakdown	Shotgun
Bucket	Old, raggedy car
Bud	Marijuana
Bullet	One year in prison
Bumpin Titties	Fighting
Busted, popped a cap	Shot at someone
Buster	A young guy, fake gang member, wanna-be
Busting	Involved in a fight with fist or weapon
Check it out	Listen to what I say
Chill out	Relaxing, hanging out
CK	Crip killer
Colum	Colombian marijuana
Colors	Showing gang membership

Crab/E-Rickett/Krab	A derogatory name for the Crip gangster
Crack	Rock cocaine
Cragard down	Low-rider type vehicle
Cuzz	Crip fellow gang member
Cuzzin	Cripping gangstering
D	Dope
Deuce-Deuce	22-caliber handgun
Do a Ghost	Leave the scene
Double Deuce	22-caliber gun
Down	Cool, willing to do what's necessary
Down for mine	Ability to protect self
Drag, Mack, Rush	Ability to sweet talk girls
Draped	Person wearing lots of jewelry
Drive by	Shooting from a moving vehicle
Drop a dime	Snitch on someone
Deuce and a Quater	Buick 225 vehicle
Du Rag	Handkerchief, cloth
Dusted	Under the influence of PCP
Eight-ball	A quarter-size ball of cocaine
Esseys	Friends
Everything is everything	It's alright
Flake	Powder cocaine
Folk	BGD's nickname
Four Five	45-caliber gun

Fresh	Latest style/trend
G-ride	Gangster ride/stolen vehicle
Gang Banging	Gang members fighting, intimidating, assaulting, drinking, partying, defending turf, sporting colors
Gat	Gun
Gauge	Shotgun
Get down	Fight
Gig	Gathering, party, event
High roller	Successful drug dealer
Holding down	Controlling turf, area
Homey/Homeboy	Fellow gang member
Hood	Neighborhood
Hustler player	Not into gangs, strictly out for money
In the mix	Involved in gang activity
Jacked up	Stopped and searched by police
Jacked up	Beat up, assaulted, get in one's face
Jammed	Confronted, get in one's face
Jim Jones	Marijuana joint laced with cocaine and dipped in PCP
Jive	Used instead of five by BGD's

Jumped in	Initiated
Kicking back	Relaxing, killing time, hanging out
Kicking it	Partying, socializing
Kool	It's alright
Laces	Chrome, spoke rims
Lady	Girlfriend
Let's bail	Let's leave
Lit up	Shot at
Loc	Loco/Crip
Lok	Loco/Blood
Main man	Best friend/backup
Making bank	Making money/usually illegal
Man	Cop
Mark	Wanna-be gang member
Monte C	Monte Carlo vehicle
Mud Duck	Ugly girl
Nine	9 mm handgun
OG	Original gangster
One time	One-man patrol car
One time	One police
On the pipe	Free basing cocaine
Packin	Carrying a gun
PK	Piru killer
Packing	Possession of a weapon
Piru	Players in red uniform
Player	Soley interested in girls
Primo	Marijuana joint laced with cocaine

Playboy bunny	Vice Lord symbol/tattoo
Put 'em in check	Discipline someone
Rag	Color of gang handkerchief
Red eye	Hard state
Ride	Car
Ride on/rode on	Go to another neighborhood in vehicle to attack other gangs
Righteous	True, affirmative answer, straight
Rock	Crystallized cocaine
Rock star	Female who performs sexual acts for cocaine
Set	Subgroup of larger gang
Sherm,Wick,Liquid Juice	PCP
Six Deuce	62
Slippin	Showing signs of weakness
Slob	Derogatory name for a Blood gangster
Snow	Powder cocaine
Sprayin	Shooting in a rapid fire
Squab	Fight, argue
Stall it out	Stop doing what you are doing
Straight up	Telling the truth
strapped	Carry a gun
Strawberry, Head hunter	Female who performs sexual acts for cocaine

Talking head	Argue, wanting to fight, talking smack, aggressive talking
Trey eight	38-caliber handgun
Trip	Too much, something else
Up on it	Knowledge, knowledge of drug scene, successful drug dealings
Uzi	Israeli sub-machine gun automatic or semi-automatic
Vice Lord	BGD's enemy (Chicago-based)
Vicky Lou	BGD's derogatory term for Vice Lords
Wacked	High on PCP
Wave	Short, close cropped haircut
What it "B" like Blood	Greeting
What it "C" like Crip	Greeting
What's up	What's going on, what's happening
What's up folks	BGD's greeting

VARIOUS GANG HAND SIGNALS

Family Bloods

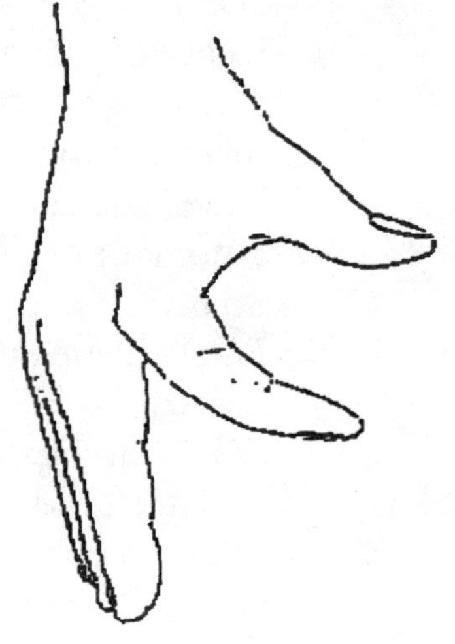

Playboy Gangster Crips

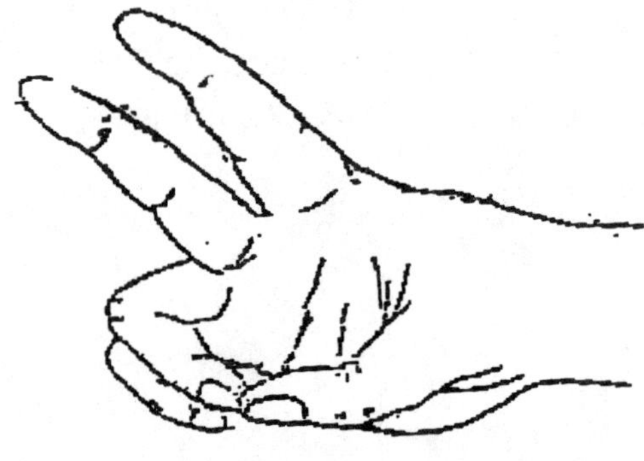

Piru Bloods

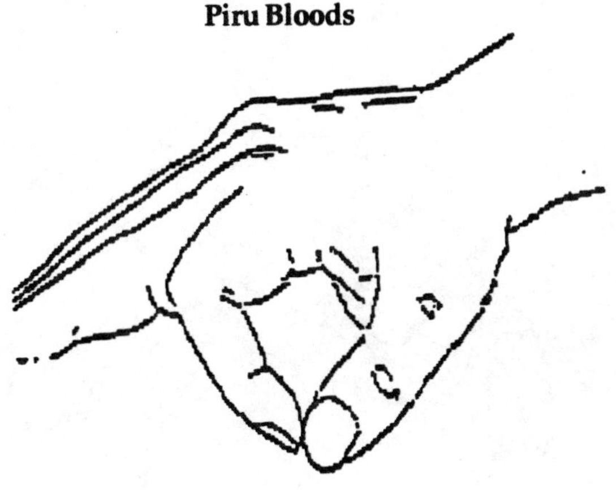

Compton Crips

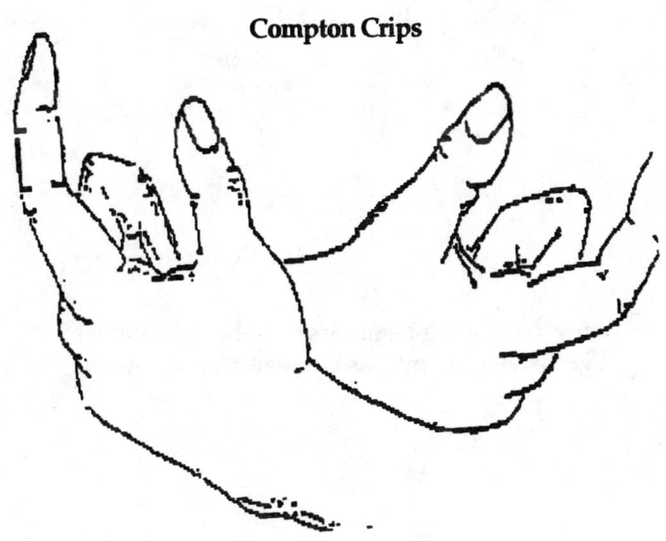

<u>TATTOOS</u>

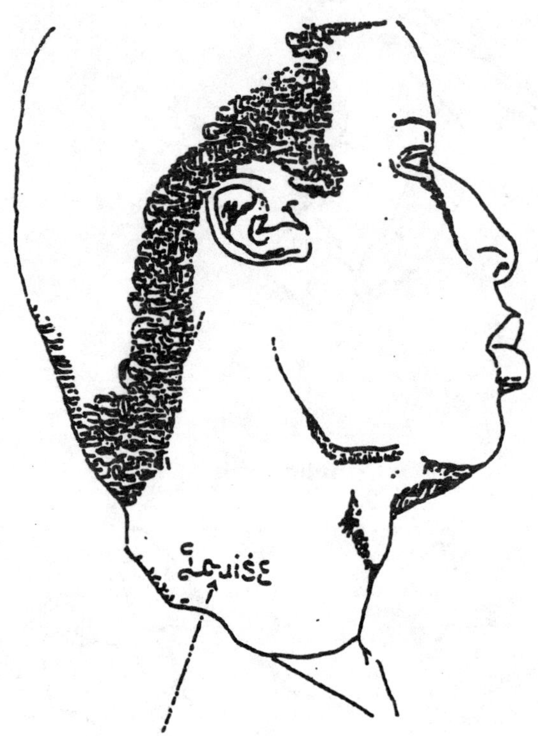

Some of the gang members have been found with girls names or initials tattooed on their necks.

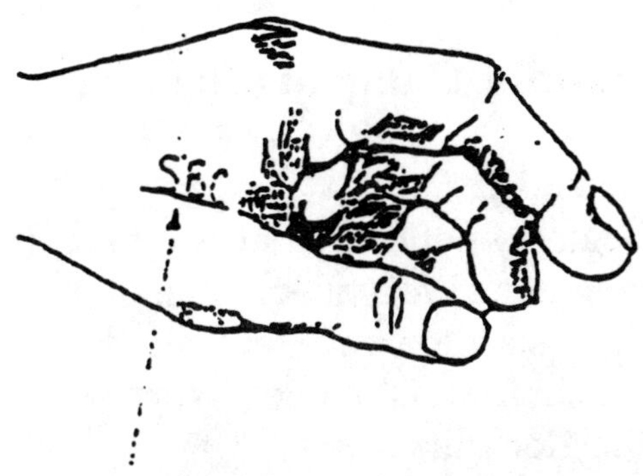

Tattoos can be on either hand.
Example: "Santana Block Crips" (SBC)

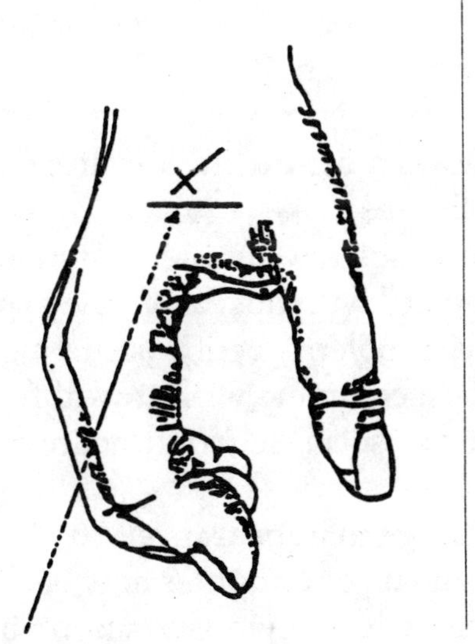

Tattoo Location

Signs of Possible Gang Involvement

• Changing friends.

You will begin to notice that at one time in your son or daughter's life, you knew all of their friends. Now you start to notice that you do not know any of their friends' names, where they live or what they look like.

• Difficult to communicate with.

Your son or daughter becomes argumentative when you talk about friends, new styles of clothing and becomes overly sensitive in accounting for their activities.

• Shows a distinct lack of interest in any family activities.

Your son or daughter's grades begin to slide downward with no reasonable explanation. Discipline problems begin occurring at school, as well as a complete withdrawal from any sort of athletic or social school functions.

• Change in appearance.

Your son or daughter now begins to dressing all one style. Previously acceptable clothes are ridiculed, cast aside or no longer worn. The clothing may become monotone in color, i.e. all red or blue. The clothing may also start to become monontone in subject, i.e. heavy metal. Hair style also becomes subject to drastic change, as well as jewelry.

- Personal graffiti.

Similar to graffiti that appears on walls, this graffiti will appear on items such as school notebooks, clothing, personal items, and bedroom walls. This graffiti will often be their street name or gang logo.

Indicators of Gang Involvement

- Radical new hair style or dress style.
- A group of new friends who have the same hairstyles and clothes style.
- Not associating with long-time friends.
- Overly secretive about friends and activities.
- Change in hours spent when with new friends (i.e. not coming home after school, which child used to do).
- Change in places frequented with new friends (i.e. going to public parks late at night or different clubs).
- Just "cruising" with new friends in vehicles (i.e. not going to the movies or parties, but just riding around).
- Use of alcohol and or narcotics.

- Possession of firearms, other weapons or narcotics.
- Going out with an unusually large group of friends (i.e. two cars with 15 friends).
- A new fear of the police.
- Phone threats to the family from rival gangs (or unknown people) directed against the child.
- Lower grades at school, discipline problems at school and at home, and cutting classes.
- Loss of interest in school, sports and other normal activities.
- Graffiti on or around your residence.
- Frequent injuries caused by fighting (caused by knives, clubs, fists, boots and guns).
- A false sense of bravery — brags that he and his friends are too tough to "mess" with — that no one can hurt him.

Preventing Gang Involvement

- Know your children's friends.
- When your children are going out, know where they are going.
- Talk to teachers and counselors at school.
- Set rules and limits and enforce them.
- Be aware of radical changes in attitude,

behavior, friends, dress style and hair style.
- Encourage hobbies and sports, or other legitimate out-of-school interest.
- Get involved with your children.

Helpful Tips for Parents

1. Remember to set aside special time for just you and your child. Make that time the most important thing you do daily or weekly.

2. Understand the difference between appropriate discipline and vengeance. Do not lash out at your child, no matter what the provocation. Wait until you are no longer angry or afraid, then apply discipline. Do not burn the bridges that connect you with your child.

When disciplining, be sure that consequences are timely, fair and reasonable, and both related and proportional to the issue at hand. It helps if discipline can be agreed upon by parent and youth. Dialogue and respect are the keys to any relationship.

3. Remember that perception is unique to the individual, and that each child is an individual. Work to establish and maintain communiction with your child. Be careful not to assume that

you and your child understand one another. Always check perceptions.

4. Construct your family constellations such that your child has a meaningful role within the family. Be sure that he/she feels needed and value. Again, check perceptions. Never assume.

5. Establish and clearly articulate family values and norms. Demonstrate and talk about these often. Create opportunities for your child to demonstrate them as well.

6. Praise your child. Catch him/her doing something right. Create avenues for your child to succeed. Always celebrate success.

7. Form liaisons with extended family, neighbors, community members, school personnel, and law enforcement. Make sure that you and your child know these people and that they know you. It is your responsibility to raise your child, but success is more likely if you do not try to do it in isolation.

8. Know your child's friends and their parents — not just their names, but some details. Know where your child is, and who he/she is with. This isn't prying, it's your job.

9. Seek out parenting literature, parent support groups, any and all resources which may help

you with your parenting experience. Know where to turn when you need help.

10. Educate yourself about the issues facing youth these days.Talk with your child about these issues without being judgmental or accusing. Be a resource for your child.

11. Remember that mistakes are wonderful opportunities to learn. Allow yourself and your child to have such opportunities without shame, blame or guilt.

Why Gangs Occur

Now that we've discussed "what" gangs are and given you a physical description of the various gangs, it is important to have an understanding of the psychological makeup or the "why" of gang involvement.

The motivation to become gang involved is often a complex web of issues which is compounded by a number of factors, including but not limited to the following:

- A child's family history
- Home life/environment
- Race and or ethnicity
- Abuse, neglect history
- Learning and behavioral disabilities resulting in poor academic performanc

- Poor self-esteem
- Inability to trust or feel safe
- Feeling of constant rejection in various social atmospheres
- Self-fulfilling prophecy of "being a loser" due to prior labeling
- Alcohol and other drug abuse
- Feeling a loss of control of one's life
- Desensitization to violence due to glamorization and increased violence through various forms of media (i.e. movies, T.V., music and music television)
- Glamorous lure of the gang lifestyle
- Lack of successful experiences in the mainstream
- Feeling or perception that no other options exist for getting one's needs met

The combination of these and other factors can be as varied as the individual, but virtually all stem from a desire to fill unmet needs in the person's life. It is important to think of gangs in terms of a "verb" and not a "noun". These are kids with problems, they are not the problem.

CHAPTER FIVE

Taking it to the Streets

What is evangelism?

"It was he who gave some to be apostles, some to be prophets, some to be evangelists, and some to be pastors and teachers."

(Ephesians 4:11)

Evangelism is a gift from God given to men. These men are commissioned by God to go out into the world and proclaim the gospel (i.e. the good news) of salvation to the unsaved and to help establish a new work in a city. When the gospel is proclaimed it always carries with it the offer of salvation. (Romans 1:16, 17)

The New Testament gives us a clear understanding of what real evangelism is about. Let's take Philip for instance. When he preached the gospel of Jesus Christ, many were saved and baptized in water. There were signs, miracles, healings and deliverance from all forms of evil spirits. Philip wanted new converts to be filled with the Holy Spirit.

Evangelism is an essential part of God's purpose for the church. The church that fails to support the ministry of the evangelist will cease to gain converts as God desires. It will become a stagnant church, devoid of growth and missionary outreach.

The church that values the spiritual gift of the evangelist and maintains an earnest love for the lost will proclaim the message of salvation with convicting and saving power!

If you believe God has called you to be an evangelist, remember there is a high price to pay. Salvation is free, but discipleship is going to cost you. As an evangelist you will be called to conduct tent, street and church revivals. You will teach seminars on evangelism, and to do so you must know your subject. Make sure God has called you to do the work of the evangelist because it is surely a great responsibility.

"Not many of you should presume to be teachers my brothers, because you know that we who teach will be judged more strictly."(James 3:1)

"We stumble in many ways. If anyone is never at fault in what he says, he is a perfect man, able to keep his whole body in check." (James 3:2)

A wise evangelist wins souls to Christ. "He who wins souls is wise." (Proverbs 11:30) And to continue to be wise, you must choose your words wisely. The evangelist who is in control of his tongue and is not at fault, he is a perfect man. (James 3:2)

"Be always willing to listen and slow to speak and slow to become angry." (James 1:19)

"A gentle answer turns away wrath, but a harsh word stirs up anger." (Proverbs 15:1)

If you want to be wise in anything in life, you must first be willing to listen and reply with a gentle answer.

Being Perfect

Never let Satan or anyone defeat you by telling you that you are not living 100 percent perfection in anything. If you are a Christian and you do not use profane language, commit adultery, steal, worship idols, perform witchcraft, hate and are not jealous, but if you love, you have joy, peace, patience, you are faithful and self-controlled, you have to be living 100 percent in at least one of these categories.

I am pastor over evangelism at Silver Lake Chapel, but I also perform in other areas such as playing the drums, singing, and playing the bass guitar with one of the worship teams. I'm not hitting 100 percent in those areas, but as pastor over evangelism, I am surely hitting the 100 percent mark on the rating scale in that area.

Surprising as it may seem, we can be perfect and still make mistakes. For example, if you go out to the car lot and buy yourself a beater you can expect it to break down. So when it does, you are not surprised. The same is with a sinner. You should not be surprised when they sin. Why? Because they are sinners. However, if you buy a brand new Lincoln Town Car from the showroom floor with no miles on it, you do not expect this car to break down. But as you know, sometimes they do. What started out to be a perfect car ended up having a bad electrical system. The difference between the beater and the Lincoln is the beater was bought "as is," just like a sinner coming to Christ. The Lincoln has a warranty and can be taken back to the dealership. It's the same with a Christian. If I make a mistake in evangelism, I have a warranty in Jesus. Praise God!

Only redeemed sinners can tell the lost about Christ. If you have never had a new Cadillac, never driven a new Cadillac, you don't know how a new Cadillac drives. But if you have one and you drive it all the time, chances are you would be able to tell someone about the luxurious drive of a new Cadillac. Too many people are trying to tell everybody what to do and they have never experienced it themselves.

"How then shall they call on him in whom they have not believed? And how shall they believe in him in whom they have not heard? And how shall they hear without a preacher? And how shall they preach unless they are sent?" (Romans 10:14-15)

The Scriptures clearly explain themselves. Only one who has been redeemed by the Lord can minister to a sinner about the Lord.

All unbelievers must first have faith. "Faith is the substance of things hoped for, the evidence of things not seen."(Hebrews 11:1)

Another word for substance is realization and another for evidence is confidence. Faith is the realization of something and the confidence that you will have the received object. This is what a sinner on the streets needs before he or she even thinks about accepting Jesus as their personal savior. We do not need to give people on the streets religion. We need to give them hope!

"For we were saved in this hope, but hope that is seen is not hope: for why does one still hope for what he sees." (Romans 8:24)

People must first have hope in their lives which is received by faith.
- There can be no calling without believing or trust.
- There can be no believing or trust with out hearing.
- There can be no hearing without preach ing.
- There can be no preaching unless the preacher has a commission to preach.

"Faith comes by hearing, and hearing by the word of God." (Romans10:17)

Faith

- Triumphant faith demonstrates the nature of the only kind of faith that is acceptable to God.
- It is demonstrated when we are in our worst situation.
- It is this type of faith that believes in spiritual realities;
- That leads to righteousness,
- Seeks God and believes in his promises,
- Has confidence in his Word (Jesus Christ),
- Rejects the evil spirit influences of this world,
- Seeks a heavenly home,

- Perseveres in testing,
- Blesses the next generation,
- Refuses sin's pleasures,
- Performs mighty acts of righteousness,
- Suffers for God,
- And does not return to the country which they left.

Why Should We Evangelize?

"But you shall have power when the Holy Spirit has come upon you; and you shall be witnesses to me in Jerusalem and in Judea and Samaria, and to the ends of the earth." (Acts 1:8)

God has commanded us to evangelize. Jesus told the apostles that the Holy Spirit was to come upon them to give them supernatural powers that would make them effective witnesses throughout the world. The first opportunity the apostles had to witness was in their own home town. And afterwards, they went out to the mission fields. As Christians it is important to take care of home before spreading abroad. Love must first begin at home.

The first seven chapters of the book of Acts tell us of the evangelization of Jerusalem. The next three chapters cover the evangelization of Judea and Samaria. There were many other cities that were evangelized and these are covered from the 11th chapter through the end of the book of Acts. When we evangelize we are showing our love for God. Jesus told Philip, "If you love me keep my commandments." (John 14:15)

I remember when I first met Julia who became my wife. I witnessed to others about her wherever I went. I told people how pretty, mature, and athletic she was. Why did I do all these things? Because I loved her. Just remember when you first accepted Jesus into your life. You couldn't help but feel the unexplainable love of Jesus. The love that never fails. (I Corinthians 13:8)

There are so many hurt and lost people in this world who need to know Jesus. The same conditions exist in your very own neighborhood.

"For all have sinned and fall short of the glory of God." (Romans 3:23)

Falling short means to lack or be without. Two things that are very important in this Scripture is that we have all sinned and fallen short. Not one person is exempt. It is very important that we understand that there are a lot of people in our own neighborhoods who need to be saved from sin.

Being Effective

If you are to be effective in evangelism, you must pray and fast. If you are just sitting around doing nothing, you will not have the power or wisdom to evangelize. My mother always told me, "If you pray you will stay, and if you fast you will last."

You must also be led by the Spirit and not self. Do not approach people on the streets with a religious attitude but with love and peace. Do not be so full of the Spirit that you cannot see the person.

"For the spirits of the prophets are subject to the control of the prophets. For God is not a God of disorder but of peace."(I Corinthians 14:32-33)

There are Christians who are using self-inspired tongues to evangelize others. Let me explain. Acts 2:4 says, "All of them were filled with the Holy Spirit and began to speak in other tongues as the Spirit enabled them." Please understand, it is O.K. to speak in tongues as long as the Holy Spirit is doing the speaking through you. There are a lot of tongue-talkers who are saying only vain words such as "Rob'e rob'e, "He tie my bow tie" (He-ta-ma-bo-ta) and "should of bought a honda" (shudda-bot-ta-hunda). The next thing you will hear is "Yabba Dabba Do" or Scoobee-Do."

If you are going to be an effective evangelist, you must follow the leading of the Holy Spirit.

"God desires all to be saved and to come to the knowledge of the truth." (I Timothy 2:4)

"Nor is there salvation in any other, for there is no other name under heaven given among men by which we must be saved." (Acts 4:12)

The last reason why we should evangelize the street is because someone once shared their faith with you. It might have been your best friend, a family member or a co-worker. You should be willing to do what others have done for you.

In the city of Everett where I live, if I want to go south to evangelize in Tacoma, I have to go through Lynnwood (Judea), Mountlake Terrace (Samaria), Seattle and Federal Way (the end). Before I even get to Tacoma, and if I am going to be an effective witness and stay on the course God planned for me to get to Tacoma, I must start in Everett (Jerusalem/home).

But if God chose to send me on a different route, it does not matter because I still have to start at home. The question most people ask is, "Why should I evangelize my community? "Because we are leaving the home mission field to go to the mission field. I am not saying don't go overseas to evangelize on the mission field. I am saying start overseeing home before you go overseas. Don't stop preaching. Just drop the "p" out of preaching and start reaching.

How Should I Evangelize?

You must be able to clearly give the simple facts of the gospel without getting deeply involved with religious and theological arguments. "For God is not the author of confusion, but of peace." (I Corinthians 14:33)

Philip, who was an evangelist, showed how to do this when he dealt with a sinner in the desert. "Then Philip opened his mouth and beginning at the Scripture preached Jesus to him." (Acts 8:35) This passage of Scripture is talking about the Ethiopian eunuch. Philip did not preach himself, nor did he preach a denomination. He preached Jesus. Many people are so busy trying to influence everyone else with their doctrines, they forget the simple process of biblically-sound doctrine. To be successful as an evangelist you have to avoid arguments and stick to the basic issues of man's sin and Christ's death, burial and resurrection. Stay with the basics!

Before God can grow your church, you have to want your church to grow. "I can do all things through Christ who strengthens me." (Phillipians 4:13) God does not want you to struggle with the growth of your church. He wants you to be successful.

Eleven Ways to Have a Growing Out-reaching Church

1. If all the sleeping folks would wake up.

    "And that knowing the time, that now it is high time to awake out of sleep for now is our salvation nearer than we believed." (Romans 13:11)

2. If all the lukewarm folks will fire up.

    "I know your works, that you are neither cold nor hot. I wish that you were either one or the other. So because you are lukewarm, neither hot nor cold, I am about to spit you out of my mouth." (Revelation 3:15-16)

3. If all the dishonest folks would confess up.

    "Confess your faults one to another, and pray for one another that you may be healed." (James 5:16)
    "He that covers his sins shall not prosper." (Proverbs 28:13)

4. If all the disgruntled folks will sweeten up.

"Pleasant words are as an honeycomb, sweet to the soul and health to the bones."
(Proverbs 16:24)

5. If all the discouraged folks will cheer up.

"Be of good courage and he shall strengthen your heart." (Psalm 31:24)

6. If all the depressed folks will look up.

"I lift up my eyes to the hills. Where does my help come from? My help comes from the Lord, the maker of heaven and earth. (Psalm 121:1,2)

7. If all the estranged folks will make up.

"Therefore, as God's chosen people, holy and dearly loved, clothe yourselves with compassion, kindness, humility, gentleness and patience. Bear with each other and forgive whatever grievances you may have against one another. Forgive as the Lord has forgiven you." (Colossians 3:12-13)

8. If all the gossipers will shut up.

"For we hear that there are some which talk among you disorderly, working not at all, but are busybodies." (II Thessalonians 3:11)

9. If all the dry bones will shake up.

"The hand of the Lord was upon me, and carried me out in the spirit of the Lord." (Ezekiel 37:1)

10. If all the soldiers will stand up.

"Endure hardness, as a good soldier of Jesus Christ." (II Timothy 2:3)

11. If all the church members will pray up.

"This then is how you should pray; our Father in heaven hallowed will be your name, your kingdom come, your will be done, on earth as it is in heaven. Give us this day our daily bread, forgive us our debts as we have forgiven our debtors. And lead us not into temptation, but deliver us from the evil one." (Matthew 6:9-13)
"Then Jesus told his disciples as a parable to show them that they should always pray and not give up." (Luke 18:1)

When Should I Evangelize?

Asking when I should evangelize is just like asking when should a sinner accept Jesus Christ.

The Bible is very clear throughout Scripture as to when you should evangelize. TODAY!

"In an acceptable time I have heard you, and in the day of salvation I helped you." (II Corinthians 6:2)

In the Old King James version of the Bible, the word helper is "succored" and in the Greek as a word is Boe'the'o. The first half of the word Boe' means to cry and Theo' means to run. When Boe'the'o is put together it means to run and cry for help. As a Christian you should always be ready to go and rescue a sinner from going to hell or help someone who is in need, because that is what God has done for you.

Every time a baby cries in the early morning hour, it is usually because it is hungry. The crying triggers the milk in the mother to start flowing. This is how it should be for you as a Christian. Whenever you see someone in need of help it should trigger the power of the Holy Spirit in you to go witness and help them.

"But you shall receive power when the Holy Spirit has come upon you; and you shall be witnesses to me in Jerusalem, and in Judea, and Samaria, and unto the ends of the earth." (Acts 1:8)

The main reason we should evangelize every day is because someone is always crying out in need. It does not matter if they are an alcoholic, drug addict or abuser, because it is all sin and a cry for help. People who are practicing sin do not know if they are even going to be living the next day. This is why now is always a good time to evangelize.

"Do not boast about tomorrow, for you do not know what tomorrow may bring forth." (Proverbs 27:1)

"Come now you who say, today or tomorrow we will go to such and such a city spend a year there, buy and sell, and make a profit. Where as you do not know what will happen tomorrow. For what is your life? It is even a vapor that appears for a little time and then vanishes away. Instead you ought to say, if the Lord wills we will live and do this or that. But now you boast in your arrogance. All such boasting is evil. Therefore to him who knows to do good and does not do it to him it is sin." (James 4:13-17)

Whenever you go to evangelize someone and tell them that they should accept Jesus in their life today because tomorrow is not promised to them, they might tell you that tomorrow is not promised to you either. Your response as a Christian to anyone about your eternal or present life is what Paul said, "To live is Christ, and to die is gain." (Phillippians 1:21)

"Count it all joy when you fall into various trials." (James1:2)

The Greek word for trial is "peiramos" which has two meanings:

- Inner impulse to evil temptation

- External adversities.

"To be absent from the body is to be present with the Lord." (II Corinthians 5:8)

And if you suffer as a Christian sometime during your life the Bible says, "Count it all joy when you fall into various trials, knowing that the testing of your faith produces patience." (James 1:2-3)

When you are going through a trial in your life, remember it is just a test of your faith. In the book of Job, Job had everything taken from him. His wife even told him to curse God and die, but Job got an "A+" on his test because he got back what he had lost and more.

I think sometimes that God could have been bragging about Job to the devil and allowed the devil to try and get Job to turn from God. He did not achieve his goal. Praise the Lord! God might be bragging on you and your faith will be tested so you can have endurance to endure a trial as a good soldier for Christ.

In spite of the trials that come with evangelizing the lost, there are great rewards to be realized at the end of it all. Winning souls may not be trial-free, but we need to know that the Lord will not allow us to be burdened beyond our capacity to endure it. The devil has a primary weapon that he uses against us disciples of Christ. As soon as we set out to work for the kingdom, Satan begins to whisper thoughts of fear and dread into our ears. However, for those who persist and RESIST, there will be an enormous blessing when we hang in there and evangelize and disciple others to the end.

Remember a good disciple practices what he is taught after receiving what is caught. Focusing on the prize (souls saved), has been the thrust of this book, and the practice of being quick to listen, slow to speak, slow to anger, and not permitting "religion" to get in your way, will change your life.

The Apostle Paul is a good role model for us modern day Christians. He witnessed everywhere — on sinking ships — in prison at midnight ("But at midnight Paul and Silas were praying and singing hymns to God, and the prisoners were listening to them." Acts 16:25), and spent the rest of his life (after meeting Jesus) talking to people about the Living God...and bringing them the good news. You can too.

I pray that this book has been an inspiring instrument in helping you become the Christian worker God desires for you to be. I encourage you to evangelize anytime, all the time, any place and in all places. May the Lord be with you.